MW00888450

Never Invite a Seagull to Lunch

By Carolyn LeComte

Illustrated by Julianna DiPaolo, Sophia DiPaolo,

And Dylan Piontkowski

Additional input from "Imaginator Apprentices"

Violet, Colton, and Sienna Piontkowski

@2015 Carolyn LeComte with CreateSpace

You're going to the beach – YAY!
While your grownups pack towels, blankets, beach umbrella, cover-ups, sunblock, snacks, lunch, water, pails and shovels – phew – there are things you can think about to help make everyone's trip to the beach a fun day. And if you all have a great experience, you're sure to return many more times.

Always wear sun block. Someone may mistake you for a lobster if you don't.

Ouch!

Bring pails and shovels to build sand castles, moats and shopping malls. Pails are also good for collecting things like those icky horseshoe crab shells your mother doesn't want near her. Maybe you can make her happy with a colorful rock.

Mommy looks funny.

Enjoy all the sights at the beach, even though you may think someone's bathing suit is too bright, or too big, or just downright silly. Everyone has their own taste – enjoy all the different colors and styles. After all, everyone is there to have fun, not to be criticized.

Be careful not to splash strangers. That lady may not want to get her hair wet. (Though why she came to the beach and expected to keep her hair dry is a mystery.)

O-o-oh! My hair!

Throwing sand doesn't make people happy. For some reason, they get very annoyed when sand gets all over them, their food, their towels, their blankets . . . at the beach. Go figure.

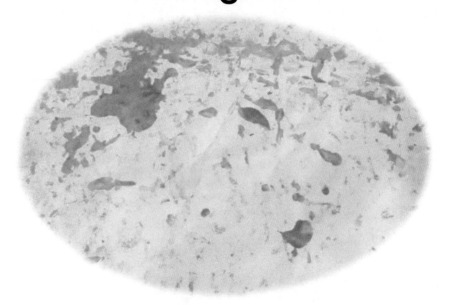

Everything is pretty, covered with sand.

If the beach rules permit throwing balls and Frisbees, make sure you are far enough away from others so they aren't hit by what you're throwing. Making people mad at you is not your goal here.

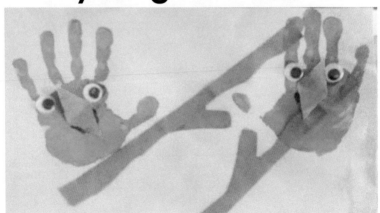

Hey! Be Careful!

If you are making a lot of noise and splashing around in the water while you are having fun, make sure you are not distracting the lifeguard. You may wind up being pulled from the water by your hair or a foot or something. Don't joke around and yell "Shark!" You may be banished from the beach. But if you do get into trouble in the water, make a loud fuss so the lifeguards can come to your aid.

Burying someone in the sand is not good. The sand is very heavy and can make it difficult for a person to breathe. Hands and feet can be buried, though. (Not heads, silly!)

Who's that?

Always look where you are going. With people lying on blankets and sitting on low chairs all over the place, you have to pay attention where you are stepping. Besides, it's more fun to see where you're going than where you've been.

Look out!

Never invite a seagull to lunch. And watch out, because they invite themselves to share your food. Keep your eats in a zippered bag or closed ice chest. They love chips, Cheetos and all kinds of goodies. They will run away with the whole bag if they can. "People food" is not good for the birds, so in many places there is a fine to be paid if you feed them. If you cause your grownups to have to pay a fine, you'll be lucky to have another beach day before you're out of high school.

Good-bye (Mr.) Chips!

Do not go in the water without a grownup, or at least stay near your grownups and always let them know where you will be. Listen to their rules about water safety and obey them. They want to go home with the same number of kids they came with.

5 people on the beach = 5 people going home
(The SAME people)

Wrap yourself in a towel when you come out of the water, and stay that way until your lips return to their normal color. For some reason, blue lips scare grownups.

A blue beak is no fun, either.

Drink plenty of water and healthy stuff. Being in the sun all day dries up the water in your skin and body. It could make you feel tired and sick.

Keep healthy!

Stash the trash in the proper waste barrel. Don't bury it in the sand or throw it in the water or let it blow away or leave it on the beach. And don't pretend it's not your job to help clean up. The next time you come to the beach you will like how clean it is.

What a mess!

After a terrific day enjoying the sun, sand, and water, everyone is content and looking forward to coming back.
And if you've followed the suggestions in this book, your grownups will be happy to spend another "day at the beach" with you!

Kristin Rennie, DVM, Unsung Hero

Kristin Rennie is a New Hampshire veterinarian who, while vacationing at the New Jersey shore with family and friends, had the unique opportunity to respond to a wildlife emergency with not a moment to spare.

While taking her customary morning solo walk along the beach, Kristin noticed something happening in the water where a great deal of thrashing was going on. She saw a seagull struggling against something that was pulling him down under the waves, where he would surely drown in a matter of minutes. Without hesitating, Kristin waded and sloshed out to the distressed bird, only to find he was tangling with a fishing line. The hook was embedded in the bird's nares (his nostrils) and threatening to do much damage to the panicked gull.

Kristin tried to stop the bird's flailing while shouting to the few people on shore to see if the lifeguard had some kind of cutting tool. But no one had anything that would work. She managed to tuck him under one arm in spite of the ceaseless waves begging the breath from the struggling bird. Our hero managed to work the hook out of the bird's nostril, paying no attention to the continued biting that left her arms scratched, bleeding, and bruised. With one huge wing-flap, the rescued animal took off and soared into the sky, with no sign of injury.

Kristin was truly a life-saver, but she didn't stop her efforts there. Noting that the hook still was in position to harm another animal, even a human, she continued trying to dislodge the line from the sand and rid the area of that danger. Without anything with which to cut the hopelessly-stuck line, Kristin resorted to the only tool she had left—her teeth. She was able to break the line that way. (Warning – kids, do not try this at home! Your parents do not want to pay those huge dental bills and you really don't want to be the only kid in school with false teeth—or no teeth, permanently.)

But Kristin risked her teeth to save another animal, or person, from an injury, perhaps even worse than the seagull had suffered. Even though he was in distress, that seagull was the luckiest bird around that day, because our hero, Kristin Rennie, was there to save him, and she did so with no thought to her personal safety.

There isn't a better way to end this book than with such an uplifting story of dedication, respect, and love for all living things. Bravo, Doctor Kristin!

Made in the USA
Middletown, DE
05 January 2020